The Battle of Britain

Alex Woolf

HODDER
Wayland

An imprint of Hodder Children's Books

THE WORLD WARS

© 2003 White-Thomson Publishing Ltd

Produced for Hodder Wayland by
White-Thomson Publishing Ltd
2/3 St Andrew's Place
Lewes
BN7 1UP

Series concept: Alex Woolf
Editor: Anna Lee
Designer: Simon Borrough
Maps: The Map Studio
Consultant: Neil de Marco
Proofreader: Philippa Smith

Published in Great Britain in 2003 by Hodder Wayland, an imprint
of Hodder Children's Books.

Woolf, Alex
    The Battle of Britain. - (The World Wars)
    1. Britain, Battle of, 1940 - Juvenile literature
    I. Title II. Lee, Anna
    940.5'4'211

ISBN 0 7502 4013 X

Printed in Italy by G.Canale & C.S.p.A., Turin

Hodder Children's Books
A division of Hodder Headline Limited
338 Euston Road, London NW1 3BH

Picture Acknowledgements
AKG 12, 30, 31, 35, 38; Camera
Press cover; Corbis 8, 15, 16, 19,
24, 42, 47; Hodder Wayland
Picture Library,17, 22, 29, 34;
Hulton Archive 54, 58-59 Mary
Evans Picture Library 6, 25, 37,
56; Newark Military Pictures 7, 44;
Popperfoto 4-5, 13, 18, 23, 26,
27, 28, 32-33, 40, 43, 45, 49, 50,
51, 52-53, 57; TRH 10-11, 36,
41, 46.

Contents

Chapter One:
Scramble!

It was 13 August 1940, at the height of the Battle of Britain. The pilots of 238 Squadron were in the dispersal hut of their sector station at Middle Wallop in Hampshire when the phone rang. It was Operations ordering them to scramble. They put down their playing cards and mugs of tea and dashed over to their planes, where the waiting ground crew helped them into the cockpits. Within minutes the twelve Hurricanes were in the sky heading for Portland where they were to intercept a raid of over a hundred enemy aircraft.

As they approached them, they could see the German planes stacked up in layers, with the bombers below, and the fighters, who were there to protect them, above. Sergeant Pilot Eric Seabourne lined up a Messerschmitt Bf 109 in his gun sight, put his thumb on the firing button and kept it there until he saw smoke trailing from the Messerschmitt's wing. Minutes later, he hit another one. Then a cannon shell hit his radiator, sending the oil temperature gauge climbing. He heard a bang and the engine stopped dead. Still under attack, some bullets hit the fuel tank just in front of him, starting a fire in the cockpit.

RAF fighter pilots race to their machines which are being prepared for take off. Pilots would already be wearing their lifejackets in readiness for the order to scramble.

Seabourne decided to get out. He detached his safety harness, oxygen and radio, then pulled at the hood. It would only open a few inches, having been damaged in the attack. The temperature in the cockpit was now unbearable. Seabourne's clothes were scorched, his wrists and face were burnt, and his goggles were melting on his face. The Bf 109s on his tail continued to fire at him, and then the wing to his left fell off. The aircraft turned upside down, and Seabourne, no longer strapped in, hit his head on the underside of the hood. The hood fell away, and Seabourne felt himself falling through the air. At 5,500 metres, the cold air soon brought him to his senses.

'The only survivor'

'I suppose it sounds as if we are having a great time - well I suppose we are really - I'm realizing an ambition, but it's a bit tough to see fellows wiped off one by one ... of the five officers, myself included, who were at Cranwell together, I am the only survivor ... a successful scrap puts me on top of the world - but I won't deny it has its frightening moments.'

George Barclay, quoted on www.battleofbritain.net

He waited until he had reached the top of the clouds and then opened his parachute. A minute later, he splashed down in the sea. With his burnt hands, he managed with difficulty to inflate his life jacket. Luck was with him, and an hour later he was rescued by a warship, and then taken to a nearby naval hospital. Eric Seabourne eventually recovered from his injuries. He was luckier than some: Sergeant Tony Marsh, a fellow pilot from 238 Squadron, did not return that day.

CHAPTER TWO:
Britain Stands Alone

In June 1940, Britain faced one of the gravest crises in its history. Since September 1939, the armies of Adolf Hitler's Nazi Germany had been sweeping relentlessly through Western Europe, conquering country after country. Hitler's seemingly unstoppable forces were now poised in northern France, just 33 kilometres from Dover, ready to launch an attack on Britain. The British people feared the worst. If the *Luftwaffe* (the German air force) could achieve air supremacy over the Channel and southern England, then nothing could prevent the German army from invading. At this critical moment, the defence of Britain depended almost entirely on the fighter squadrons of the Royal Air Force (RAF). Between July and October 1940, they waged an heroic air battle against the *Luftwaffe*. The Battle of Britain, as this conflict became known, came to be seen as one of the most crucial encounters of World War II.

'The Führer's purpose'

'Naturally, it matters a lot what the British expect the Führer's purpose to be in fighting their country ... Can the British ... swallow their envy and pride enough to see in him not the conqueror but the creator of the new Europe? If they continue to wallow in their present pigheadedness then God help them.'

Walter Hewel, Hitler's Diplomatic Liaison Officer, 30 June 1940, quoted in Len Deighton, *Battle of Britain*

Conquerors turned tourists: German soldiers enjoy the view from Montmartre in newly occupied Paris. The French capital fell on 10 June 1940. Twelve days later, the French government surrendered.

The RAF and the Battle of France

World War II began in September 1939 when France and Britain declared war on Nazi Germany following the German invasion of Poland. In the spring of 1940, Hitler launched his Blitzkrieg, or Lightning War. Led by armoured panzer divisions on the ground and supported by the *Luftwaffe* in the air, the *Wehrmacht* (the Germany army) invaded Denmark, Norway, Holland, Belgium, Luxembourg, and finally northern France, in just ten weeks.

The RAF had been involved in a limited way from the start of the war, with attacks on the German naval fleet and a few aerial battles with *Luftwaffe* fighter squadrons. However, its war really began on 10 May 1940 with the German invasion of France. The invading forces were supported by around 1,400 aircraft. The *Luftwaffe* quickly established air superiority by destroying most of the French air force's 275 fighters and 70 bombers while they were still on the ground.

The RAF sent in a force of 400 fighters and bombers to help in the struggle to save France. These included Battle and Blenheim bombers, an older class of aircraft and no match for the high-speed modern German fighter planes. The British bombers were supported by six squadrons of Hurricanes (a RAF squadron is made up of about sixteen planes) and a few Gladiator fighter planes. However, no effective system had been set up to direct them to where they were needed.

weblinks

For more information on the opening stages of World War II, go to
www.waylinks.co.uk/ worldwarsbattleofbritain

A Hawker Hurricane is refuelled and rearmed before being sent back into action over Dunkirk. During the Battle for France, the RAF suffered the loss of 435 pilots – killed, missing or captured – and 959 planes.

Home Defence Dwindles

By 15 May the RAF had lost 205 aircraft. Four more squadrons of Hurricanes were sent to France as reinforcements. The French prime minister, Paul Reynaud, urged the British to send more. He told Winston Churchill, the British prime minister, that ten more squadrons were necessary if the Battle of France was to be won. The RAF leadership believed that Britain required a minimum of 52 fighter squadrons in order to defend its own shores against a German invasion. Thanks to the RAF's commitments in France, there were now only 36 squadrons available for home defence.

On 16 May a written appeal was made to the British government by Air Chief Marshal Sir Hugh Dowding. Dowding was commander-in-chief of Fighter Command, the wing of the RAF responsible for the air defence of Britain. He wrote: '… if the Home Defence Force is drained away in a desperate attempt to remedy the situation in France, defeat in France will involve the final, complete and irremediable defeat of this country.' Despite Dowding's letter, ten more Hurricane squadrons were sent to France, reducing Fighter Command to 26 squadrons – exactly half the force that was thought essential for the protection of Britain.

Hurricanes flying in formation over the British countryside.

Dunkirk

The British Expeditionary Force (BEF), which had been sent to help in the defence of Europe in the first few weeks of the war, soon found itself encircled in north-eastern France by the fast-moving German forces, and forced back towards the Channel port of Dunkirk. Between 26 May and 4 June, the Royal Navy, with help from merchant seamen and civilian boatmen, evacuated the remains of the BEF from Dunkirk, while under heavy bombardment from the *Luftwaffe*. The troops waiting to embark, and the ships off the coast, presented easy targets for the German bombers. Only the actions of the RAF in attacking the bombers before they reached their targets prevented a massacre. In all, over 338,000 British and allied troops were rescued at Dunkirk.

The RAF at Dunkirk

During the evacuation, the fighter planes of the RAF flew continually from their bases in southern England to Dunkirk, where they attempted to intercept the German bombers before they reached the beaches. However, the distances they had to fly meant that they only had about 15 minutes' worth of fuel over the combat zone before being forced to return home. With 18 squadrons made available by Dowding, only two squadrons could patrol the coast at a time if a reasonably continuous presence was to be maintained. By contrast, the *Luftwaffe* bases were nearby in Holland and France, and they could time their bombing raids to occur in between RAF sorties. From 29 May, the patrol strength was increased to four squadrons, although this left longer intervals – up to an hour – when the *Luftwaffe* had the freedom of the skies. The RAF became very unpopular with the soldiers waiting to be evacuated below, as it seemed to them they were doing little to prevent *Luftwaffe* attacks. However, the RAF did manage to down more than 240 German planes during the nine days of Dunkirk, for a loss of 170 aircraft.

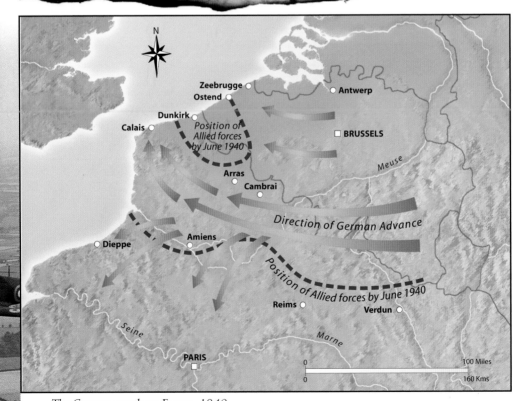

The German attack on France, 1940.

> ### 'We shall never surrender'
>
> On 4 June, as the Dunkirk evacuation ended, Churchill summed up the British spirit in a famous speech of defiance:
>
> *'We shall defend our island, whatever the cost may be. We shall fight on the beaches, we shall fight on the landing grounds, we shall fight in the fields and in the streets, we shall fight in the hills: we shall never surrender ...'*

Operation Sealion

Within three weeks of the Dunkirk evacuation, France had fallen. Britain stood alone in Europe against the Nazi onslaught. Hitler believed the British would surrender. When it became clear towards the end of July that the British, under the inspiring leadership of Churchill, had chosen to fight on, Hitler gave orders for the preparation of an invasion – Operation Sealion.

However, even at this stage, Hitler remained unsure about the necessity of a full-scale seaborne invasion and occupation. He had always admired the British, and he believed that German and British interests need not necessarily be in conflict. Attacking Britain or its empire had never been part of Hitler's plans. The occupation of Western Europe had been carried out mainly in order to remove the threat from the west before embarking on his main goal: the expansion of the German empire eastwards and the destruction of the communist Soviet Union. The stubbornness of Britain in remaining hostile after June 1940 was an irritation to Hitler because it forced him to delay his plans in the east.

On 13 July, the German general staff gave Hitler their plans for Operation Sealion. The target date for the invasion was set for mid-August, later postponed to 17 September. The invading force would be transported and supplied by a fleet of 155 transports and 3,000

weblinks

For more information on the Dunkirk evacuation, go to
www.waylinks.co.uk/ worldwarsbattleofbritain

Preparations for Operation Sealion on the coast of France.

barges and smaller boats. During the initial 'assault phase' 90,000 men would be landed, with airborne forces parachuted in. Their job would be to secure beachheads on three fronts around Ramsgate, Brighton and Portland. A second consolidating force would consist of 260,000 men. The plan was to occupy the country in stages – advancing first from Portland to Bristol, and then to occupy the south east of Britain on a line between Portsmouth and the Thames estuary, before taking London and the remainder of southern Britain.

However, before Sealion could be launched, Britain's air defences would have to be put out of action. The RAF would have to be defeated, so that the German Navy could carry the invading forces safely across the Channel. The responsibility for this was given to the *Luftwaffe*. On 1 August 1940, Hitler gave the following order: 'The *Luftwaffe* is to overpower the RAF with all the forces at its command, and in the shortest possible time.'

weblinks

For fascinating first-hand accounts from senior German officers revealing the background to Operation Sealion, go to
www.waylinks.co.uk/ worldwarsbattleofbritain

CHAPTER THREE

The Threat from the *Luftwaffe*

When Hitler became chancellor of Germany in 1933, plans were immediately drawn up for an expansion in German air power. Hermann Goering, one of the most senior members of the Nazi government, was placed in charge of a newly created air ministry. With the help of his deputy, Erhard Milch, Goering secretly launched a new air force, the *Luftwaffe*. Hitler, with his dreams of conquest, urged speed in the development of the *Luftwaffe*. By the end of 1934, 584 planes had been built, and by the outbreak of war, this number had risen to 3,750, with a monthly output of 700 aircraft.

A German aircraft factory in 1939. Germany had just 36 planes in 1932, yet by the outbreak of war the Luftwaffe *was one of the most powerful air forces in the world, employing over 400,000 people.*

The Germans tended to view their airforce mainly as 'aerial artillery', attacking enemy forces on the ground ahead of the advancing *Wehrmacht*. For this role they built a great number of single- or twin-engined bombers and dive-bombers. To their cost, they never developed a long-range bomber with a heavy bomb-load capacity, as the Allies did, which could have carried their attacks long distances behind enemy lines.

The Aircraft

For the attack on Britain, the Germans made available some 1,300 bombers and dive bombers, and about 900 single-engined and 300 twin-engined fighters. The bombers included the highly effective Junkers Ju 88A, which could achieve the impressive speed of 458 kph with a full bombload, making it a difficult target. By contrast, the Dornier Do 17Z, known as the 'Flying Pencil', could only manage a maximum of 416 kph, was very vulnerable to fighter attack, and carried a smaller bombload. The German Heinkel He 111 was equally slow, though better armoured, and it carried almost twice the Dornier's bombload. The symbol of the German Blitzkrieg was the Junkers Ju 87B, or Stuka. This single-engine dive-bomber terrified enemy ground troops with its screaming siren and near-vertical dives. However, its low speed and lack of armour made it an easy target for enemy fighter planes.

weblinks

For more information on the bombers and fighters of the *Luftwaffe*, go to **www.waylinks.co.uk/ worldwarsbattleofbritain**

Hermann Goering interrogating a pilot just returned from a raid on England. Goering was a popular figure, but also highly self-indulgent. He spent a large part of the Battle of Britain in his luxurious mansion, Carinhall, north of Berlin.

Hermann Goering

Goering was born in 1893, the son of a retired government official. During World War I he became one of Germany's most famous fighter pilots. Goering joined the Nazi Party in 1922, and when the Nazis achieved power, Goering was made president of the Reichstag (the German parliament) and prime minister of Prussia. During the 1930s, as commander-in-chief of the Luftwaffe, he oversaw a massive expansion in Germany's air power. By June 1940, after the Luftwaffe's early triumphs in the war, Goering was at the height of his power and prestige. However, he was not a military thinker, and he fatally underestimated the strength of the British defences during the Battle of Britain. As Germany's fortunes waned during the war, so did Goering's prestige. In 1946 he committed suicide, after being condemned to death at the Nuremberg war crimes trial.

Fighter Planes

To protect the bombers, a force of fighter planes was developed. In 1935, the *Luftwaffe* placed an order for the Messerschmitt Bf 109, a light, high-speed, aerodynamic monoplane fighter. This proved a fine aircraft and the Germans' most potent weapon during the Battle of Britain. A fighter was also developed with a longer range to accompany bomber attacks. This was the twin-engined Messerschmitt Bf 110, which although slower and less manoeuvrable than the Bf 109 was still an effective fighter.

weblinks

For more information on how the *Luftwaffe* was organized, go to
www.waylinks.co.uk/ worldwarsbattleofbritain

How the Luftwaffe *was Organized*

The total force of bombers and fighters that the *Luftwaffe* had assembled by September 1939 included over 1,000

The organization of the Luftwaffe, *August 1940.*

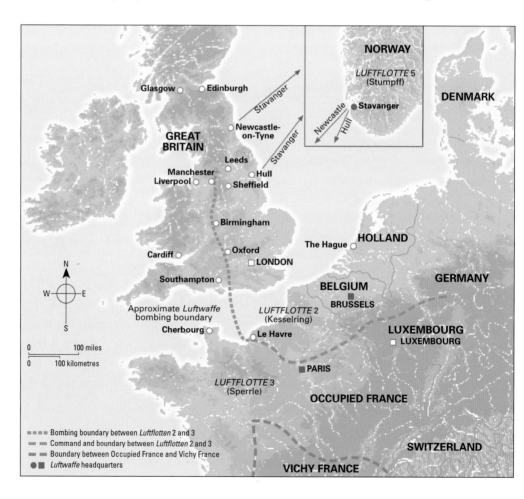

Bf 109s, 195 Bf 110s, and 1,270 He 111, Do 17 and Ju 88 bombers. This force was organized into *Luftflotten*, or air fleets, each containing a full range of fighters and bombers, and each with its own command and support structure.

For the planned attack on Britain, three air fleets – *Luftflotten* 2, 3 and 5 – were deployed in an arc stretching from Norway to the Cherbourg peninsula in northern France. *Luftflotte* 2 was stationed in airfields in north-eastern France and Belgium, while *Luftflotte* 3 was located in north-western France, and *Luftflotte* 5 in Norway. A line was drawn down the centre of England; *Luftflotte* 2 was to operate east of this line and *Luftflotte* 3 to the west; *Luftflotte* 5 was assigned to north-eastern Britain.

Each *Luftflotte* was divided into about three *Fliegerkorps* (Air Corps), which were split in turn into several *Geschwader*, units made up of either bombers (*Kampfgeschwader*), or fighters (*Jagdgeschwader*). The *Geschwader* contained about 120 aircraft and were divided into three *Gruppen*. Each *Gruppe* included three *Staffeln* consisting of about twelve aircraft each, and was headed by a *Stabschwarm* of about four aircraft.

The Messerschmitt Bf 109 E.

Messerschmitt Bf 109 E

This plane was arguably the greatest fighter aircraft on either side during the Battle of Britain. The aircraft designer Willy Emil Messerschmitt created the Bf 109 with a small, light and aerodynamic frame. In 1938, it was redesigned to incorporate a more powerful Daimler engine. This new model, the Bf 109 E, affectionately known as Emil by its pilots, had a top speed of 560 kph, and it could climb and dive at greater speeds than British fighters. The Bf 109 carried two 20 mm cannon in its wings, and two 7.9 mm machine guns mounted on the engine. Its one drawback was its limited range – about 640 kilometres – which meant that during dogfights over England in the Battle of Britain, pilots only had around twenty minutes in the combat zone before having to return to base, often leaving their bombers dangerously exposed.

CHAPTER FOUR:
Britain's Defences

The threat of air power came to dominate military thinking around the world during the 1920s and 1930s. At the time, there did not appear to be any means of effective defence against planes dropping bombs from the air. This fear was expressed by the British prime minister Stanley Baldwin when he said, 'the bomber will always get through'.

These words, spoken in 1932, were a fairly accurate description of the situation at the time, and if the Battle of Britain had been fought in that year the result might have been very different. The fighters of the early 1930s had little advantage in terms of speed over bombers.

At the 1936 Annual Royal Air Force Show at RAF Hendon, biplanes fly in formation over a car park crowded with spectators.

No effective early warning systems had yet been developed, and anti-aircraft guns could be evaded by bombers simply by flying higher.

The Royal Air Force

The only defence against air attack, it was claimed, was to build a bomber force the equal of your enemy, to act as a deterrent. In Britain, this cause was championed by Sir Hugh Trenchard, chief of the air staff and commander of the RAF between 1919 and 1929. Under his leadership and on into the 1930s, the largest portion of the RAF's budget was spent on developing its bombers. Fighters were seen as less strategically important, and in 1936, the RAF possessed just 13 fighter squadrons out of a total force of 42.

However, by this time, the belief that the bomber was invulnerable had started to erode. New men had risen to the top of the RAF, including Sir Edward Ellington, who became chief of the air staff in 1933, and Sir Hugh Dowding, chosen to run the newly created Fighter Command in 1936. These men believed that it was possible for Britain to defend itself against air attack.

Air Chief Marshal Sir Hugh Dowding

Dowding was born in 1882, the eldest son of a school headmaster. He joined the Royal Flying Corps in 1914 and was decorated for his service in World War I. In July 1936 Dowding was made commander-in-chief of Fighter Command. It was his organization of Britain's air defences between 1936 and 1940, and his insistence on retaining a minimum number of fighter squadrons for home defence once war broke out, that was responsible more than anything else for Britain's ultimate victory in the Battle of Britain. Despite his success, Dowding's leadership of Fighter Command was under constant attack during the summer of 1940 by rivals in the Air Ministry and the RAF, who favoured a different approach to air defence, and he was dismissed from his job in November 1940.

SERVE IN THE WAAF WITH THE MEN WHO FLY

A recruitment poster for the Women's Auxiliary Air Force. The force grew from 1,700 members at the outbreak of war to around 180,000 by 1943.

17

The RAF Expands

Alarmed by the expansion of the *Luftwaffe* during the 1930s, the British government began devoting more resources to developing the RAF. Thanks to the insistence of Ellington and Dowding in the RAF, and the support of Defence Minister Sir Thomas Inskip, fighter planes were given a higher priority. The number of fighter squadrons grew from thirteen (about 208 planes) in 1936, to thirty-nine (about 624 planes) in September 1939. At the same time, efforts were made to increase the number of fighter pilots. Training schools were increased from six to eleven, and 2,500 trainee pilots were recruited. This rapid expansion in the number of planes and pilots was crucial to the success of Britain's defence in 1940.

The Supermarine Spitfire

The Supermarine Company were successful builders of high-speed seaplanes during the 1920s. One of their planes, the S.6B, broke the world air-speed record in 1931, flying at 651 kph. That year their chief designer, Reginald Mitchell, turned his attention to building a fighter plane. He employed the same principles that had

New recruits at the RAF Cadet College at Cranwell, Lincolnshire, in 1934. Here trainee pilots would learn about the theory of flying, engines, physics, armaments, British history, and other subjects.

weblinks ↖

For more information on the history and development of the Spitfire, as well as those who built and flew it, go to **www.waylinks.co.uk/ worldwarsbattleofbritain**

already brought him success with the S.6B, using a slim fuselage of light metal construction. He combined this with a revolutionary rounded-edge wing of great strength despite its narrow depth, which decreased air resistance and therefore increased the aircraft's speed. The aircraft was fitted with the powerful and reliable Rolls-Royce Merlin engine, and eight Browning machine-guns spaced along the wings.

The Spitfire versus the Messerschmitt Bf 109 E

As two of the most potent and respected fighters on either side during the Battle of Britain, many comparisons have been made between the Spitfire and the Bf 109 E. The Bf 109 E was the smaller plane, making it more difficult to hit. Its top speed of 560 kph matched that of the Spitfire, and it could climb and dive faster than the British plane, although Spitfire pilots claimed that in an extended dive they could gain on it. However, the Bf 109 E was less manouevrable than the Spitfire, and less easy to fly, with a cramped cockpit and restricted vision.

The Spitfire flew successfully for the first time in March 1936. Its unique shape immediately marked it out as an aircraft of great beauty and grace, much loved by the pilots who flew it. It was fast, powerful and highly manouevrable, and the bubble canopy gave the pilot excellent visibility. The Air Ministry placed an order for the plane in 1936, and by July 1940, Fighter Command possessed 13 Spitfire squadrons. Mitchell died in 1937, aged 42, and so never witnessed the glorious role his aircraft was destined to play in World War II.

The Supermarine Spitfire: sleek, swift, manoeuvrable and strong. One pilot compared it to driving a sports car.

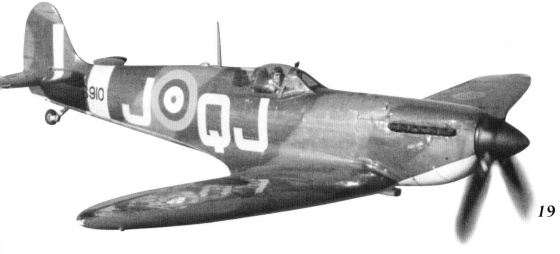

The Hawker Hurricane

The Hurricane was a single-seater fighter created by Sydney Camm, the chief designer at Hawker. With its wood and fabric construction, strengthened by a metal-tube framework, it was a more conventional aircraft than the all-metal Spitfire. This made the Hurricane simpler to manufacture, and easier to patch up after being damaged in battle. Powered by a Rolls-Royce Merlin engine, it flew for the first time in November 1935. In June 1936, the Air Ministry placed its first order, and by July 1940 there were 24 Hurricane squadrons available for operation.

In terms of numbers of aircraft used, the Hurricane was the most important British fighter during the Battle of Britain. Over 1,715 Hurricanes took part in the battle, and they were responsible for shooting down about 80 per cent of the German aircraft credited to Fighter Command. However, the Spitfire is the more famous plane, partly because of its greater speed (the Hurricane's top speed was 520 kph), the beauty and revolutionary nature of its design, and the fact that it remained Britain's foremost fighter throughout the war, while the Hurricane was downgraded to a fighter-bomber role from 1941.

Fighter Command

Fighter Command was not just responsible for fighter squadrons, but also for Britain's overall defence network, including intelligence gathering, early warning systems and anti-aircraft defences. From 1936, Dowding began organizing Britain's defences. He divided the country into four groups: 11 Group covered the south east; 10 Group the south west, while 12 and 13

The Ops Room

At the centre of Britain's defences throughout the battle was the Operations Room (Ops Room) at Stanmore, north west of London. Each group also had its own Ops Room, and information from around the country about incoming raids flowed into Stanmore and was then passed to the Ops Room of the relevant group.

Each Ops Room was dominated by a large table containing a map of Britain. Women of the WAAF (Women's Auxiliary Air Force) used croupiers' rakes to move coloured counters on this map to show the position and direction of the raiders, enabling group commanders to decide which sector station to commit to battle.

weblinks

For more information on the structure of Fighter Command, go to
www.waylinks.co.uk/ worldwarsbattleofbritain

Groups were responsible for the Midlands and the north of Britain. These groups were sub-divided into sectors, each with their own sector station (or airfield). Fighter Command headquarters fed information about incoming raids to the groups, and the main job of the groups was to deploy the squadrons in their sectors appropriately in order to intercept the raiders. Information about raids came from three main sources: the radar stations, the observer corps and the radio monitoring service.

The organization of Britain's air defences.

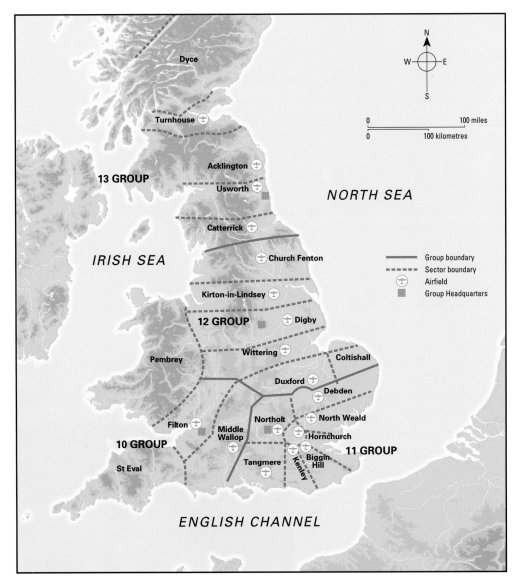

Radar

The British began experimenting with the detection of aircraft by radio waves in 1935. It had already been known for some years that radio waves bounced back off distant aircraft. However, it was the British scientist Robert Watson-Watt who first suggested that this 're-radiation' of radio waves might be used to detect the position and location of aircraft. A government committee chaired by the scientist Sir Henry Tizard agreed to fund the research, and in 1936 the first practical tests of radar were carried out at Biggin Hill near London.

Biggin Hill

The scientists and staff at Biggin Hill began developing a system in which ground controllers using radar could plot the distance and speed of incoming planes with sufficient accuracy to enable successful interceptions by fighter squadrons. Encouraged by the results, the Air Ministry authorized the building of a further seventeen radar stations along the southern and eastern coastline of Britain. This was known as the Chain Home range, and it was later supplemented by the more sophisticated 'Chain Home Low' stations, installed to detect low-flying aircraft.

The use of radar changed the whole nature of air warfare, making it possible for a defending country to accurately anticipate a bomber attack early enough to intercept it. In 1940, Britain possessed the most advanced radar early warning and fighter direction system in the world, making the difference between a successful defence and almost certain defeat.

weblinks

For more information on Britain's radar early warning system, go to **www.waylinks.co.uk/ worldwarsbattleofbritain**

A pair of Chain Home radar masts on the British coast. Radar stations could detect incoming aircraft up to 192 km away when flying above 3960 m. Their range became progressively shorter when planes flew lower.

Observer Corps

Radar could give early warning of an incoming raid when it was still at a distance, but human observers were required once the raiders had crossed the English coastline in order to identify the types and approximate number of German aircraft involved. This was the job of the Observer Corps. Observer posts were established along the coast – about 30 to each group. Each post consisted of between 14 and 20 trained observers. They passed information by telephone to their parent Observer Corps centre, which would plot the direction of the raid, and then feed this to the ops room of their group. The group ops room informed Fighter Command Ops Room in Stanmore. Group ops then decided which squadron should be scrambled to intercept.

Radio Monitoring

The Germans generally maintained radio silence during raids, but radio communication was often unavoidable between *Luftwaffe Staffeln* (squadrons) and their bases. The 'Y' Service, based at Cheadle in Cheshire, was responsible for listening in on German radio transmissions. These could either be in the form of ordinary voice transmissions, known as radio-telephony (R/T), or in coded transmission (W/T). As well as passing on the content of the messages, the 'Y' Service could also inform the Ops Room about the direction and location of transmissions to warn them of a raid when it was still out of radar range.

Air Vice Marshal Sir Keith Park

Keith Park, a 44-year-old ex-pilot from New Zealand, was the commander of 11 Group, responsible for the defence of the south east of Britain, which was to face the brunt of the enemy's attacks throughout the battle. His job was to decide which squadrons to commit to meet a raid. This called for a fine sense of judgement and timing. With limited resources at his disposal, Park had to consider which raids were important and which were minor attacks or feints (mock attacks intended to draw the enemy from the true point of attack). While Dowding's greatest achievements lay in preparing Britain's defences before the battle, once the battle was underway, the running of Fighter Command was mostly down to the group commanders, and particularly Park.

Air Vice Marshal Sir Keith Park was widely praised for his calm judgement and skill in the deployment of limited resources. 'If any one man won the Battle of Britain, he did,' said Lord Tedder, Chief of the Air Staff, in 1947.

CHAPTER FIVE

The Pilots

In the 1920s and 30s, the RAF sent its best pilots to the bomber squadrons. This under-investment in fighter pilots meant that by 1940, Fighter Command had to rely heavily on reservists (non-professional pilots) and part-timers to fly its planes. About a quarter of the RAF fighter pilots who took part in the battle fell into this category, including many who were under-trained or some years past their peak.

Despite the popular image of RAF pilots as coming from upper class backgrounds, only about 200 of the 3,000 Battle of Britain pilots were public school educated. However, these pilots with their silk-lined flying jackets and expensive sports cars gained a disproportionate amount of public attention, causing resentment from pilots of humbler origins.

Fighter Command was undoubtedly strengthened by the large numbers of pilots from British Empire or Commonwealth nations such as Australia, New Zealand, South Africa, Canada and Rhodesia, as well as from the countries of occupied Europe, especially Poland, Czechoslovakia, Belgium and France. A small number of American pilots also took part in the battle.

Czechoslovakian pilots in England in 1940. Many of these men had also fought in France. In all, 87 Czech pilots flew during the Battle of Britain, and seven were killed in battle.

The Poles and the Czechs, many of whom had lost their homes and families, fought with the greatest ferocity. One Czech pilot, Sergeant Josef Frantisek, had notched up 17 kills in the battle before his death in October 1940, making him Fighter Command's second highest scoring pilot.

The German fliers were generally more experienced than their British counterparts, many having already fought in Europe during the Blitzkrieg and earlier in the Spanish Civil War (1936-39). They were also very well trained. The German training schools had for many years been producing 800 pilots a month, compared to just 200 a month being produced by the RAF in 1939. At the start of the battle, morale among German pilots was high, and relations between officers and lower ranks was less formal than in the RAF.

A Luftwaffe aircrew prepare for a bombing mission. The morale of the German fliers was very high at the start of the battle. After their successes in Spain, Poland, Norway, the Low Countries and France, many believed they were invincible. They also had the advantage of all offensive forces: the ability to choose where and when they would strike.

In Training

The famous Battle of Britain pilot, Richard Hillary, had these memories of training:

'We learned of the advantage of height and of attacking from out of the sun; of the Germans' willingness to fight with the height and odds in their favour and their disinclination to mix it on less favourable terms; of the vulnerability of the Messerschmitt 109 when attacked from the rear and its almost standardised method of evasion … a half roll, followed by a vertical dive right down to the ground. As the Messerschmitt pilots had to sit on their petrol tanks, it is perhaps hard to blame them.'

Quoted in Richard Hillary, *The Last Enemy*

During the summer of 1940, the British people braced themselves to meet the invasion that seemed to many to be inevitable. In every part of the country, soldiers and civilians helped in the construction of pillboxes, anti-tank ditches, and barricades at road junctions and military bases. The beaches of expected landing sites were covered with barbed wire, and over 200,000 people were evacuated from the towns of the east and Kentish coasts. Blackouts were imposed at night in case of night raids by enemy bombers, and instructions were given for the building of air raid shelters. Despite the new restrictions, morale remained high.

Firing the Sea

Many schemes were suggested for repelling an invasion. One of the more bizarre ideas to be considered was setting fire to the English Channel. A Petroleum Warfare Department was set up in June 1940 to look into ways of igniting a blaze on the sea and the beaches as a means of blocking an invading force. Experiments using fuel pipes with holes punched in them were carried out with unpromising results, and the idea was soon set aside.

Two little girls with buckets and spades can find no way around the barbed wire barrier that keeps them from the beach. In all, 11,500 anti-invasion obstacles were placed around the coastal areas of Britain during 1940.

weblinks

For more information on the Home Guard go to
www.waylinks.co.uk/ worldwarsbattleofbritain

The Army

The civilian population might have been less confident of victory had there been a fuller awareness of the state of Britain's defence forces. Following many years of under-investment and the disastrous experience of the BEF in Europe, the British Army was in a poor situation. Infantry divisions usually consisted of about 13,600 men, but by the summer of 1940, Britain's fifteen infantry divisions were all at less than half their original strength, and its one armoured division was incomplete. The infantry divisions were badly under-equipped with only one-sixth of their normal quantity of field and anti-tank guns. For transport, they depended on buses driven by civilian drivers. There were fewer than a thousand tanks in the entire country.

With the return of the BEF from Dunkirk, the number of divisions was increased to 27. However, the shortage of guns and equipment remained acute. During the summer, arms production was stepped up and the organization of forces was improved, so that by September, the army was in a better position to meet at least the first wave of a German invasion.

Local Defence Volunteers

In May 1940, the government called upon civilians to join a newly created force called the Local Defence Volunteers (LDV), which would form small fighting units in every town and village in the country. In the event of a full-scale German invasion, these units were expected to act as a first line of defence before regular troops could be drafted in. In August the LDV was renamed the Home Guard.

Members of the Home Guard on parade. The War Office had not initially planned on a citizen's army for home defence, but were provoked into it by the appearance up and down the country of bands of civilians arming themselves with shotguns.

The Home Guard

With most men of fighting age already in the forces or else in jobs vital to the war effort (such as government jobs, manufacturing and construction), the appeal was aimed mainly at older men. The response was far bigger than the government expected, and within a month 750,000 men had volunteered. Very few of this number could be armed with rifles, so the majority found themselves issued with outdated or improvised weaponry. Nevertheless, the Home Guard undertook valuable guard and lookout duties that would otherwise have had to be carried out by regular soldiers. Their presence also gave local communities a sense of direct involvement in the war effort.

Weapons of the Home Guard

Home Guard weapons included old shotguns, swords, clubs and staves, and pieces of gaspipe with bayonets welded on the end. There was even a cutlass platoon in Essex. The Home Guard had some unique weapons, some of which were allegedly more dangerous to the operator than the enemy. These included the No. 74 ST Grenade (sticky bomb) – so dangerous that the regular forces refused to use it. It had an adhesive coating – designed to stick to the side of a tank – that sometimes became stuck to the thrower's clothing. Once the safety lever had been released, he had just five seconds to detach himself from the bomb.

Anti-Aircraft Defences

Anti-Aircraft Command played an important part in the defence of Britain in 1940. It was the responsibility of Lieutenant-General Sir Frederick Pile, who worked closely with Dowding and Fighter Command. In the summer of 1940, there were just 1,200 anti-aircraft (or ack-ack) guns placed at strategic points around Britain, near military bases and key towns and factories – too low a number to deal adequately with the massed raids from the continent.

Anti-aircraft gunners loading a gun at Rye in south-east England. By July 1940 Anti-Aircraft Command had only half of the heavy and less than a third of the light ack ack guns considered essential to resist a German attack. As a result many military bases and industrial areas were left unprotected.

The guns were fired in a barrage (that is with every gun firing at the same time). Each gun was equipped with a searchlight for night raids. The tracking and aiming devices on the guns were primitive and few shells ever hit their targets. However, the sound of the ack-ack guns raised morale of civilians on the ground. They also forced enemy bombers to fly higher and therefore drop their bombs with less accuracy.

Barrage Balloons

Barrage balloons were large gas-filled balloons that were tethered above important factories and towns to discourage the Germans from attempting low-level bombing or dive bombing. There were some 1,500 deployed around the country, usually flown at around 1,500 metres. They were reasonably effective, although RAF pilots occasionally flew into them in the midst of a dogfight.

Barrage balloons over London in 1940. There were 450 deployed in defence of the capital. The balloons were particularly effective against dive bombers.

CHAPTER SEVEN

The Eve of Battle

A neutral observer of the two sides in early July 1940, on the eve of the Battle of Britain, might have drawn the conclusion that Britain stood little chance of withstanding the forces ranged against it. Despite the defiant speeches of Churchill and the high morale of the British people, in purely numerical terms, the *Luftwaffe* was massively superior to RAF Fighter Command. The three *Luftflotten* comprised a total of 2,800 aircraft flown by battle-hardened pilots and crews operating from bases just a few minutes' flight across the Channel. In response, Fighter Command could muster only about 600 fighters, many flown by inexperienced and under-trained pilots.

weblinks

For a day-to-day diary of the Battle of Britain, giving details of casualties on both sides, go to
www.waylinks.co.uk/ worldwarsbattleofbritain

In this German propaganda photo from 1940, a Stuka is being loaded with bombs ready to be sent into action against the British.

However, despite their numerical disadvantages, the British were better prepared for defence than the Germans had anticipated. In July 1940 the *Luftwaffe's* intelligence group compiled a report on the RAF that underestimated the effectiveness of Hurricanes and Spitfires as fighters when compared to the Messerschmitt Bf 109. The report correctly estimated the number of RAF fighters available, but did not mention the dramatic increase in aircraft production the British had achieved by 1940, averaging 470 new planes a month over the summer. This was occurring just at the time German aircraft production was starting to decline.

Just as significantly, there was no mention in the report of radar or operations rooms, and it is clear that the Germans went into battle ignorant of Dowding's well-organized fighter direction systems. The report concluded, 'The *Luftwaffe* is clearly superior to the RAF as regards strength, equipment, training, command and location of bases …' Hermann Goering, confident after his recent victories in France, saw the forthcoming battle as another opportunity to bask in the glory of his all-conquering *Luftwaffe*.

Generalfeldmarschall *Albert Kesselring*

'Smiling Albert' Kesselring was commander of Luftflotte 2, based in north-eastern France and the Low Countries. His air fleet faced south-east England, making him Keith Park's chief adversary. As a former commander of Luftflotte 1 in the attack on Poland, the 55-year-old Kesselring had a successful track record. However, commanding close formations of dive-bombers in support of the advancing Wehrmacht was very different from facing a well-coordinated air defence system across a stretch of water. Despite this unpreparedness, he came very close to defeating Britain's defences in the south east.

Albert Kesselring, like Goering, was a strong believer in the power of bombers to overwhelm cities, having already waged successful bombing campaigns against Warsaw and Rotterdam.

CHAPTER EIGHT

The Battle Commences

The Battle of Britain did not have a clearcut beginning. Small scale bomb attacks began on Britain on the night of 5-6 June, and minor, infrequent raids continued through the rest of June and July. The Air Ministry later chose 10 July as the official start date, as this marked the starting point of heavier attacks along the Channel coast. However, for many of the pilots at the time the day seemed no busier than previous days that month.

The first phase of the Battle of Britain lasted until around 11 August. This phase has been called *Kanalkampf*, or the Channel Battle, because most of the fighting took place in the skies over the English Channel. German bombers, with fighter escorts, began attacking Allied coastal shipping as a means of luring RAF fighter squadrons into battle. The RAF responded by scrambling fighter squadrons to patrol the skies above the shipping convoys. This led to some of the first dogfights of the battle.

In most encounters RAF squadrons found themselves heavily outnumbered by German planes. For example, on 20 Hurricanes engaged in a dogfight with 40 Bf 109s off Dover, Kent at 12.30 p.m. Two hours later, eight Spitfires of 64 Squadron, sent to patrol a convoy, met 30 Ju 88 bombers escorted by 50 Bf 109s. That day, 16 German planes were lost compared to six British.

The First Kill

D. M. Crook, an RAF pilot of 609 Squadron, recalls his first kill:

'At that moment I saw dimly a machine moving in cloud on my left and flying parallel to me. I saw that it was a Ju 87. I was in an ideal position to attack, and opened fire ... at very close range ... Pieces flew off his fuselage and cockpit covering, a stream of smoke appeared from the engine, and a moment later a great sheet of flame licked out from the engine cowling and he dived down vertically ... I followed him down and saw him hit the sea with a great burst of white foam. He disappeared immediately, and apart from a green patch in the water there was no sign that anything had happened.'

Quoted in Len Deighton, *Battle of Britain*

From reports of these encounters a popular impression soon formed that a small band of British fighter pilots were holding out against the overwhelming strength of the *Luftwaffe*. However, the truth was that the low numbers of RAF fighters on patrol at any given time had more to do with Dowding's strategy of conserving his resources than a shortage of pilots and planes. Despite the fact that Park's 11 Group was facing the vast majority of attacks, Dowding maintained as large a force of fighter squadrons outside 11 Group as he did within it. Between 1 July and 11 August, British losses were 124 planes; German, 274.

A Messerschmidtt 110 is exhibited in Finsbury, North London, in October 1940. Throughout July, the capital remained untouched by the battle, and many Londoners went about their business as if there was no war on at all.

Tactics

During the early stages of the battle, the inexperience of British pilots was brutally exposed by their more seasoned German counterparts. The RAF had trained its pilots to fly in close formations of three, either in a V-shape (known as a 'vic') or in a line next to each other. This tactic proved highly vulnerable to attack from above or behind. To fly in close formation, pilots had to spend a large part of their time concentrating on avoiding collision, and consequently had less time to look out for the enemy.

Flying in their formations of three, RAF fighters were trained to attack by peeling off one by one and diving on the enemy, while firing in bursts. However, this approach depended on the enemy flying a steady course, which the Germans understandably refused to do while being shot at! When a dogfight began, it was almost inevitable that one RAF aircraft would become separated from the other two, as the planes dived and twisted around the sky. A lone RAF pilot was always in greater danger from German fliers, who tended to fight in pairs.

German fighter tactics – known as the *Schwarm* – involved flying in pairs or fours. The leading pilot of a pair was the attacker. The other pilot was the wingman, whose job was to defend the leader.

Spitfires flying in formation.

Fighter pilot Werner Molders (centre) was an inventive and original tactician. During the Spanish Civil War, flying a Bf 109 prototype, he devised the Schwarm formation. He went on to become the top German ace in the Battle of Britain.

The wingman flew low on the sun side of the leader and never departed from his side. In the case of a four, the other two pilots flew adjacent and just behind, and adopted a similar formation.

This tactic, developed during the Spanish Civil War, proved psychologically very effective, as each pilot in the partnership was free to concentrate on either attacking or defending. It was soon adopted by the RAF pilots, who called it the 'finger four', because, from above, the formation conformed to the position of the fingertips on an outstretched hand. The leader would position himself at the tip of the longest finger. His number two would be at the tip of the index finger, while numbers three and four would be at the tips of the other two fingers. Fighter Command also soon learned to fight in open, rather than close formations, as this made a squadron harder to see from a distance.

The Schwarm

The *Schwarm* tactic is illustrated in this account of a dogfight which took place over Portland on 25 August:

'*When we reached the first Ju 88s, a Hurricane squadron appeared, flying in two 'vics' with more pairs behind. At once I gave orders to attack, and broke my Staffel into pairs ... Suddenly I saw a Hurricane diving on the last Ju 88 of the formation. I followed him together with my wingman. The Hurricane opened fire at long range. Simultaneously I fired ... and the enemy broke away downwards. While I was attacking my wingman warned me that I was in danger from above and behind,... I followed the Hurricane in a dive,... I fired, and the Hurricane went up in flames,...*'

Hans Karl Mayer, 1/JG53, quoted in Len Deighton, *Battle of Britain*

CHAPTER NINE

Eagle Attack

By the beginning of August, the situation appeared bleak for Fighter Command. The pilots were very tired after repeated scrambles day after day. Radar was not giving the British too much of a head start, with the German bases so close across the water. A German plane took five minutes to cross the Channel, whereas, even with the help of radar, it took fifteen minutes for an RAF fighter to reach sufficient altitude to intercept it. The RAF had lost 118 aircraft by the end of July. These planes were being replaced, with factory production now greatly improved. Far more seriously, 80 squadron and flight commanders – Fighter Command's most experienced pilots – had already been killed.

The Germans, however, were quite confident at this stage of the fighting, believing the RAF was close to breaking point. On 1 August, Hitler authorized Goering to launch a major attack on Britain at his own convenience.

A pilot takes a well-earned rest between sorties.

After consulting the weather forecasters, Goering declared that 13 August would be the first day of *Adlerangriff*, or Eagle Attack. This time his bombers would move further inland with an all-out assault on Fighter Command itself. Goering predicted that in fourteen days the RAF would be crushed, and the way would be clear for Operation Sealion.

Radar Stations Attacked

However, before Eagle Attack could be launched, Britain's radar stations would need to be disabled. The past six weeks had taught the Germans that Fighter Command's early warning system was a lot more effective than they had originally suspected. On 12 August, the stations at Dover, Dunkirk in Kent, Rye, Pevensey and Ventnor on the Isle of Wight, were all attacked. However, the bombing was not as successful as the *Luftwaffe* had hoped. Only Ventnor radar station suffered serious damage, and three days later it was back in operation.

German aircrew put on parachutes in preparation for a mission.

Blind Britain

The attacks on Britain's radar stations temporarily blinded Britain. The *Luftwaffe* took swift advantage of this by launching raids on the RAF airfields at Lympne, Hawkinge and Manston, Kent, on the afternoon of 12 August. Corporal Wireless Operator D. G. Lee, in charge of the signals section at Hawkinge, recalled the attack:

'… the screamers started coming down out of the sky. We had no time to get out of the building to the air-raid shelters as all hell was let loose outside, so we scrambled underneath radio benches and teleprinter tables, expecting every moment to be our last.'

Quoted in Richard Hough and Denis Richards, *The Battle of Britain: The Jubilee History*

Adlertag

Goering named 13 August *Adlertag* (Eagle Day), the start of his operation to 'wipe the British air force from the sky'. For the Germans it turned out to be a day of anticlimax and confusion. The first problem was the weather. Contrary to predictions, southern England lay under thick and unbroken cloud, obscuring the bombing targets unless the bombers flew below cloud level – a very dangerous policy because of barrage balloons and ack-ack guns.

The decision was taken at 6.15 a.m. to defer *Adlerangriff* to later in the day. However, this order was not received by *Kampfgeschwader* 2 (KG2), made up of 74 Dornier bombers, which had left its base at 5 a.m., and which continued on its mission despite the absence of a fighter escort. Just after 7 a.m. KG2 broke through the cloud above the Thames estuary and bombed the coastal bases at Sheerness and Eastchurch. The RAF were soon on the scene, and five Dorniers were destroyed and six damaged.

German bombers on a raid over Britain. On 15 August, attacks were launched for the first time on Biggin Hill and Kenley, the two vital 11 Group sector stations defending London.

── **weblinks**▶ ──

For more information on the events on 13 August – *Adlertag*, go to **www.waylinks.co.uk/ worldwarsbattleofbritain**

Bailing out

RAF fighter pilot Alan Deere describes baling out of his Spitfire on 13 August:

'I had just reached Folkestone when my pursuers broke off the engagement ... Two minutes later my engine ... burst into flames. Desperately I tore my straps off, pulled back the hood and prepared to bail out ... I shot out a few feet and somehow became caught up by the bottom of my parachute. I twisted and turned but wasn't able to get either in or out. The nose ... was [now] pointing at the ground, which appeared to be rushing up at a terrific speed. Suddenly I was blown along the side of the fuselage, hitting my wrist a nasty smack on the tail. Then I was clear. I made a desperate grasp at the ripcord and with a jolt the parachute opened.'

Quoted in Alan Deere, *Nine Lives*

By mid-afternoon, the weather had improved, and *Adlerangriff* was finally launched with attacks mainly by *Luftflotte* 3 on RAF airfields on the west and central south of England. By 3.30 p.m., almost 300 *Luftwaffe* aircraft had formed over the Channel with orders to smash 10 Group, its aircraft, airfields and operations rooms.

By 4 p.m., every squadron in 10 Group had been scrambled, as the German planes separated to deal with their wide range of targets. Poor visibility prevented many bombers from finding their targets. One force of Stukas failed to find RAF Warmwell, and simply scattered their bombs on the countryside.

Some bombers became separated from their fighter escorts and were sitting targets for RAF fighters. By the end of *Adlertag*, 45 German aircraft had been destroyed for the loss of 13 RAF fighters in the air and 47 aircraft – including just one fighter – on the ground.

The Assault Continues

On 15 August, another major assault was launched. This time, *Luftflotte* 5, based in Norway, was used in strength for the first time, as well as the other two air fleets. The day was a disaster for the *Luftwaffe*, whose bomb attacks failed to destroy any vital targets: 71 German aircraft were destroyed against 29 British. Never again in the battle did German bombers risk attacking without adequate fighter cover, and never again did *Luftflotte* 5, whose bases were too far from Britain for Bf 109s, launch a major assault on Britain.

Over the following days, the *Luftwaffe* continued their attacks. In dogfights, the Bf 109s continued to outperform Spitfires and Hurricanes, and the RAF fighter pilots were reminded to focus their attention on the bombers.

weblinks▸

For more information on the 'Big Wing' theory, go to **www.waylinks.co.uk/ worldwarsbattleofbritain**

The 'Big Wing' Debate

The pressure of the *Luftwaffe's* assault led to divisions over Fighter Command's strategy. Air Vice-Marshall Trafford Leigh-Mallory, commander of 12 Group, along with his supporters in the Air Ministry, believed that Dowding and Park's strategy of sending up single squadrons to face the massed formations of German aircraft was ineffectual. He favoured the 'big wing' approach, scrambling three or more squadrons at a time in order to take on the attackers on something closer to equal terms. However, Dowding and Park both stuck firmly to the view that the British were bound to lose a battle of attrition in which each side merely sought to shoot down the maximum number of their enemy's aircraft. Fighter Command could achieve victory simply by continuing to exist, and that meant conserving their forces.

Leigh-Mallory expected to be offered command of the prestigious 11 Group during the Battle of Britain, and was resentful when this position went to Keith Park, souring his relationship with Dowding.

The battle reached its most intense phase between 24 August and 6 September, with the *Luftwaffe* focusing its assault with an even greater ferocity on the southern sector stations of Fighter Command, particularly those guarding London. The plan was to force Fighter Command to commit all its forces in a battle of attrition, which the *Luftwaffe* – with its superior numbers – must eventually win.

German intelligence believed Britain was down to its last 300 fighters, although the actual figure was around 700. However, the sheer weight and number of attacks proved exhausting, and it was during this critical phase of the battle that Fighter Command came closest to defeat.

The RAF base at Hemswell was bombed on 27 August, but the bomb didn't detonate. This photograph shows its controlled detonation, which did no damage to the station.

Fighter Command in Crisis

There were bombing raids on RAF bases throughout the south east, as well as raids on cities such as Portsmouth, Liverpool and Luton. During this intense phase, 11 Group pilots were being scrambled six or seven times per day, having been on readiness since dawn, and all were suffering from exhaustion. By 1 September, the shortage of experienced RAF fighter pilots was becoming critical. During the month of August, 286 pilots were killed or wounded out of a total number of about 1,400. This loss rate was higher than could be made good by the training units. Because of the shortage of trained men, new pilots were being brought into squadrons with only 24 hours' experience of Spitfires or Hurricanes, and were often killed on their first engagement

Dowding's intricate early warning and fighter direction system was kept operative during these dark days by sheer hard work and improvisation. Cratered landing fields were quickly repaired and tents were erected as temporary accommodation for bombed-out staff at operations rooms. However, the network inevitably suffered from the loss of power lines and telephone links.

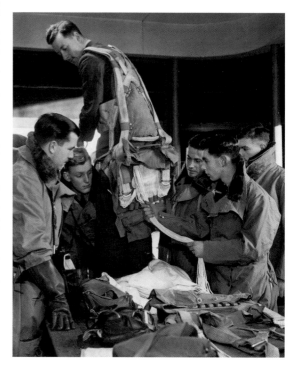

Adlerangriff had also taken a heavy toll on the *Luftwaffe*. Morale among German pilots was low. After receiving repeated assurances that the British were on the brink of defeat, it was frustrating to find themselves surrounded on every raid by swarms of Spitfires and Hurricanes. German aircrews adopted a cynical attitude to optimistic intelligence reports, joking as they approached the British coast: 'Here they come again, the last fifty British fighters.'

A group of RAF student pilots is shown the correct way to open and pack a parachute during training at an elementary flying training school. There were thirty-one such schools scattered around the country.

Morale in the Luftwaffe

Adolf Galland (III/JG26) describes the feelings of his fellow Luftwaffe *fighter pilots at the height of the battle in his book* The First and the Last: *'Failure to achieve any noticeable success, constantly changing orders betraying lack of purpose and obvious misjudgement of the situation by the Command … had a most demoralizing effect on us fighter pilots …We complained of the leadership, the bombers, the Stukas, and were dissatisfied with ourselves. We saw one comrade after the other, old and tested brothers in combat, vanish from our ranks. Not a day passed without a place remaining empty at the mess table. The reproaches from higher quarters became unbearable. We had the impression that whatever we did we were bound to be in the wrong …'*

Soldiers stand guard over the wreckage of a Junkers 88 bomber, brought down in Hertford, south-east England. Air Ministry officials noticed increasing strain and low morale among captured German pilots during late August and early September.

CHAPTER TEN

The Pilots Become Stars

During the Battle of Britain, the daring exploits of the young fighter pilots captured the public imagination, both in Britain and Germany, and they came to be seen as the most glamorous and heroic figures of the war. The duels that took place each day in the skies above southern England between the 'knights of the air' harked back to an earlier, more chivalrous form of conflict.

The propaganda of both sides tended to emphasize the romantic aspects of aerial warfare. German magazines, such as *Signal*, and British popular papers, such as *Sunday Pictorial*, portrayed their nation's pilots as clean-cut heroes, with a cheerful, devil-may-care attitude. Many pilots may have fitted this description in the early days of their experience. However, the stress and exhaustion of constant exposure to danger, and the loss of comrades, caused those who survived the first few weeks to adopt an attitude of grim determination to do their duty.

Aces High

Aces were defined as pilots who destroyed in air combat at least five aircraft. On both sides there were pilots with exceptional skills who shot down many more enemy planes than their comrades. These men were instinctive fliers, with fast reflexes and a deadly aim, enabling them to out-turn and out-dive their opponents in dogfights, so manoeuvring themselves into position to make a kill. Their skills also allowed them to evade enemy fire more successfully than the average pilot, extending their chances of survival.

British newspapers such as the Daily Sketch *played their part in the propaganda war, and were prone to exaggerate the successes of RAF pilots.*

Luftwaffe aces were much higher scorers than their RAF counterparts, mainly because they were kept on operational duties for far longer periods. The three highest-scoring German aces were Helmut Wick (56 aircraft destroyed), Werner Moelders (40), and Adolf Galland (40). The top RAF aces were E. S. Lock (18), J. Frantisek (17), and B. Carbury (15).

weblinks

For more information on Sir Douglas Bader go to
**www.waylinks.co.uk/
worldwarsbattleofbritain**

Douglas Bader

Bader, a celebrated squadron commander during the Battle of Britain, was born in 1910. He joined the RAF in 1930. Eighteen months later he lost both his legs in a flying accident. He learned to fly again using artificial legs, and rejoined the RAF in 1939. He was given command of 242 squadron during the Battle of Britain. Bader held strong views on tactics — believing squadrons should be free to make their own choices in the air - and he frequently clashed with Dowding. By 1941, Bader had shot down 23 German planes during the course of the war, making him the fifth highest ace in the RAF. In August 1941, he was shot down over occupied France. He baled out, but damaged his artificial legs on landing. He managed to escape from hospital, but was arrested and sent to the German prison camp, Colditz. Freed at the end of the war, Bader returned to Britain. He was knighted in 1976, and died in 1982.

Squadron Leader Douglas Bader on the wing of his Hurricane. During the Battle of Britain, he was an inspirational if controversial figure. On his squadron's first sortie, they shot down 12 German planes in just over an hour; Bader was responsible for downing two.

CHAPTER ELEVEN

Bomber Command

The role played by RAF Bomber Command in the Battle of Britain is less well known than the more high-profile exploits of Fighter Command. While Fighter Command defended the homeland during the summer of 1940, Britain's bombers attempted to take the fight to the enemy with regular raids on targets in occupied Europe.

Bomber Command carried out thousands of sorties against German shipping, airfields and aircraft factories. British bombers, such as Whitleys, Hampdens and Wellingtons, which were used in these attacks, were cold, uncomfortable aircraft for pilots and crew to fly in on long night-time journeys across Europe. They lacked the sophisticated navigation equipment developed by the *Luftwaffe* to allow its pilots to find their bombing targets in darkness. Yet daylight raids were highly dangerous: Fighter Command, stretched to its limits in defence of Britain, could not spare fighter escorts for all these raids, leaving bombers often defenceless against intercepting enemy fighters.

Daylight raids

Daylight raids by Bomber Command without fighter protection caused extremely high casualty rates. Seven out of twelve Hudson bombers were lost on one raid over Stavanger in Norway on 9 July. On 13 August, eleven of twelve Blenheims were lost attacking Aalborg in Denmark. These attacks were costly in lives and equipment, and did little damage to the German military and industrial machine. Yet they made the important contribution of putting areas under air-raid warning, slowing production in the factories and lowering morale.

Bombers in flight.

More effective were the attacks by Bomber Command on the invasion fleet that had begun building up at the French channel ports in early September in preparation for Operation Sealion. In 1,600 sorties during September, British bombers destroyed just over 12 per cent of the barges and troop transports assembled there, as well inflicting considerable damage to jetties, docks, roads and railway lines.

Yet arguably the most important contribution by Bomber Command to the Battle of Britain came with one of its least effective attacks. On the night of 24-25 August, the *Luftwaffe* had accidentally dropped some bombs, destined for industrial targets, on the City of London – the first time the capital had been bombed since 1918. Churchill immediately ordered a retaliatory strike, and on the following three nights British bombers were sent to bomb Berlin, the German capital. The physical damage caused by these attacks was very small. Yet Berliners – who had previously felt themselves invulnerable – were shocked. Hitler was enraged by this attack. His response led to a complete change of strategy in the *Luftwaffe's* campaign against Britain.

'The Berliners are stunned'

W. L. Shirer, an American newspaper correspondent, was in Berlin at the time of the raid by Bomber Command:

'The Berliners are stunned. They did not think it could ever happen. Goering assured them that it couldn't. Their disillusionment today is all the greater. You have to see their faces to measure it.'

W. L. Shirer, Berlin Diary, quoted in Richard Hough and Denis Richards, *The Battle of Britain: The Jubilee History*

Berliners clean up after British bombing.

CHAPTER TWELVE

The Blitz

On 30 August, at a meeting between Hitler and Goering, the German leader forcefully expressed his wish for the *Luftwaffe* to carry out attacks on the British capital in revenge for Bomber Command's raids on Berlin. On 3 September, Goering met with Albert Kesselring and Hugo Sperrle, the commanders of *Luftflotten* 2 and 3, and informed them that the main attack would be switched from the airfields of Fighter Command to London.

By 6 September, after two weeks of relentless battering, Fighter Command was close to being overwhelmed. Had Goering, Kesselring and Sperrle known this, and ordered the *Luftwaffe* to continue pressing home their attacks, the RAF would undoubtedly have been defeated within a matter of weeks. By switching the thrust of their attack to London, the *Luftwaffe* gave Fighter Command a crucial breathing space in which to recover. It was to be the Germans' biggest strategic error, and would mark a decisive turning point in the Battle of Britain.

The German hope was that an attack on the capital city would draw British fighters into battle in sizeable numbers – something they had resisted doing until now – allowing the *Luftwaffe* to finish them off in large-scale aerial battles. It was also hoped that a full-scale aerial assault on London would demoralize the people and cause administrative chaos, softening up Britain before the planned invasion.

Fighter Command knew nothing of the German change of strategy, and as far as Dowding and Park were aware, Saturday 7 September was to be another day of defending their own sector stations in the south east. Observer Corps must have been shocked at the sight of almost a thousand German aircraft, one third of them bombers, crossing the English coast at around 4 p.m.

weblinks

For more information on air raids, evacuation, rationing, and many other Home Front topics, go to
www.waylinks.co.uk/ worldwarsbattleofbritain

The alert was frantically sounded, and by 4.30 p.m. all twenty-one squadrons around London had been scrambled. In the skies above the Thames Estuary, to the east of the Isle of Sheppey, they witnessed a terrifying spectacle: a formation 2.4 kilometres high, covering 1,280 square kilometres of sky. Such an armada – the largest ever launched – could only be heading in one direction: London.

The bombers attacked along 14 kilometres of the Thames waterfront, from the East End and the docks to as far west as Kensington. There were 448 civilians killed, and thousands of firemen were drafted in from all over southern England to deal with the huge fires. Fighter Command could do little against such a huge force, and 31 fighters were lost that day, against just 39 German aircraft.

Rescue workers shift debris with their bare hands as they search for survivors after an air raid on London.

'Bang after bang'

George Turnbull was a Home Guard member on the bombing in Limehouse. He recalled:

'This first day of bombing was most dreadful. Most of us thought '... what on earth is happening, this is it ... we are finished', but of course, this was really only the beginning. Explosions were everywhere, there just was not a break, bang after bang after bang ... You would hear a whistle as a stick of bombs came down then a loud explosion as they hit factories and houses, the ground shook. Then as soon as that explosion happened, another whistle and another explosion ... this seemed to go on for hours.'

Quoted in Alan L. Putland, *Remembering the Way it Was: The Blitz of 1940*

The Climax of the Battle

During the following days and nights the raids on the capital continued. The biggest German raids came on 15 September, the climax of the Battle of Britain. By this time, a week after the ending of the airfield attacks, Dowding's forces – having flown far fewer sorties – were feeling rejuvenated. The German formations were met by much larger forces of sixty or seventy British fighters. This was because Dowding, under pressure from Leigh-Mallory, had given authorization for the limited use of 'big wings', consisting of two or more squadrons, to meet these massive German formations. The Germans lost 79 aircraft that day, the British 36.

After such devastating losses, Goering's repeated promises that the RAF was on the verge of elimination had begun to sound hollow. Furthermore, the weather was starting to worsen, and Hitler and his chiefs of staff decided that time had run out for an invasion before the winter. On 17 September, Hitler postponed Operation Sealion indefinitely.

A dogfight takes place over High Holborn in London during an increasingly rare German daylight raid on 8 October 1940.

The Germans continued to attack day and night for the rest of September. As well as the bombing of London, there were night raids on Liverpool, South Wales, Glasgow, Bristol and the north east of England. On 30 September, British fighters blocked a large German raid on the capital, destroying around fifty German planes. Virtually no bombs reached their targets, and several German officers were killed. The *Luftwaffe* leadership decided to withdraw virtually all its bombers from daylight attack.

From the beginning of October, the Germans attacked almost only at night. The RAF used night fighters to defend against nocturnal bombing raids. These were conventional fighter planes, such as Hurricanes and Defiants, that were painted black and equipped with radar to locate incoming bombers. However, the equipment did not work very well, and successful interceptions were quite rare. Only 54 German bombers were shot down during the night blitz of 1940 – 1 per cent of the bombers sent. The night fighters, the ack-ack guns with their searchlights, and the barrage balloons, were Britain's only defence against the night-time bombing raids.

Londoners shelter in an Underground station during an air raid.

Air Raids

The Blitz lasted until May 1941. London was bombed heavily. Other cities and towns were also heavily bombed, including Swansea, Cardiff, Bristol, Southampton, Plymouth, Birmingham, Coventry and Liverpool. Although many places in Britain were badly damaged during the Blitz, German bombing failed to halt munitions production. Over 30,000 British people were killed during this period – over half of them in London, which was bombed almost every night. For Londoners, the period from September to November 1940 was the worst as the German bombers attacked the capital every night for a total of sixty-seven nights.

Morale Stays High

Despite the bombardment, communities in most parts of Britain held together and continued to function. The mass panic and chaos that had been predicted before the war did not occur. In the wake of the first big raids on London in September 1940, paralysis overtook parts of the city as thousands of people stayed away from work. But as the raids continued, people became used to them, and ordinary needs, such as for wages and food, resurfaced and people ventured out again.

During air raids, people were encouraged to use public shelters or private shelters assembled in their house or garden. In reality, most people simply stayed in their homes and hoped for the best. People whose homes had been bombed – of which there were 25,000 in London alone by the end of September 1940 – lived in overcrowded Rest Centres, provided by local authorities. A Women's Voluntary Service manned the Rest Centres, providing food and arranging warm clothing for people who had been made homeless. They also assisted in the difficult task of finding people new accommodation. Six weeks into the Blitz, only 7,000 people had been re-housed.

The Air Raid Precaution (ARP) organization employed 400,000 full-time wardens to supervise air raid shelters, issue gas masks, set up first-aid posts, and help rescue the injured. An Auxiliary Fire Service, numbering 60,000, was also recruited to support Britain's 6,000 professional firefighters in dealing with the widespread fires that blazed in the cities almost every night.

Evacuation

Although many children had been evacuated in the early months of the war, the biggest evacuation from London occurred on 1 September 1940. In all 600,000 children

Vanishing Houses

Gerald Cole was a child in London during the raids of September 1940:

'The air raid warden ran along the street shouting for all he was worth, "Get in your shelters!" My sister crawled in beside me. My mother was still scrambling in when I saw the walls of the room crumbling and tumbling towards us ... I cannot remember any sound that night, just the sights – the tumbling walls, the dust and then – I could scarce believe it – the night sky! Our house had completely vanished.'

Quoted in Alan L. Putland, *Remembering the Way it Was: The Blitz of 1940*

Settling In

Irene Fisher was evacuated from Chiswick in London to Worcestershire in 1939:

'It took a while for me to settle in … Working with animals, farm life and even an orchard was a far cry from living near factories, the noise of traffic and living in rows of terraced houses … Hot baths with hot water on tap was something new as I was used to an old steel tub that hung on the back wall of the house being brought in once a week for the family bath time.'

Quoted in Alan L. Putland, *Remembering the Way it Was: The Blitz of 1940*

Mothers and children arrive at a railway station for evacuation to the country. Special timetables had to be arranged for the many extra train services. Many of the evacuees did not even know where they were going.

were evacuated to safer areas in the countryside between 1 and 3 September. The introduction of city children – many of them from slum areas – to homes in country towns and villages proved a culture shock for many of the children as well as their foster parents. Evacuees had a mixture of experiences. There were some instances of ill-treatment or lack of care. For others it was a happy time in their lives.

Although fighting would continue for several months afterwards, many consider 15 September to be the day the Battle of Britain was actually won – although this only became apparent later. After that day, the *Luftwaffe* never again confronted Fighter Command in such large numbers, and not long afterwards, daylight raids virtually ceased. With hindsight it became clear that 15 September marked the point when the Germans realized they could not defeat the RAF and gain command of the skies over Britain; British fighters were simply shooting down German planes faster than German factories could produce them.

Operation Sealion was postponed indefinitely by Hitler on 17 September. On 31 October, Churchill accepted that a German invasion that year had become very unlikely, and the British forces standing by to defend against Sealion were placed on a lower state of alert for the winter. The official end date of the Battle of Britain has since been named as 31 October. But victory was not certain at the time. Many in Churchill's government believed that the efforts of Fighter Command had merely forced a postponement of the invasion until the following year. It was not until the German invasion of Russia in June 1941 that the British government felt truly safe from invasion.

weblinks

To read an essay explaining the significance of 15 September 1940, go to
www.waylinks.co.uk/ worldwarsbattleofbritain

Pilots of the County of London Squadron.

That an epic battle had even been fought was not immediately clear to many Britons at the time. The term 'the Battle of Britain' was first used in reference to the air war in March 1941 when the Air Ministry published a best-selling account of the battle with that title. Dowding, who had by that time been forced out of his job by his enemies at the Ministry, was not mentioned in the text.

In Germany, the battle was treated even more dismissively, and its significance in terms of the overall progress of the war was minimized. Some former *Luftwaffe* pilots have even maintained that there never was a Battle of Britain, or if there was, the British did not win it. The *Luftwaffe* remained undefeated when its air fleets were transferred to the Eastern Front in 1941 in preparation for the invasion of Russia.

A Chill in the Air

Raymond Lee, United States Military Attache in London, 15 September 1940:

'This is the date after which I believe Hitler's chances will rapidly dwindle… there are faint premonitory puffs of wind from the south west and a chill in the air … there are the beginnings of a press campaign in Germany breaking the news to the people that England is to be subdued by blockade and bombing.'

Quoted in Len Deighton, *The Battle of Britain*

Casualties of the Battle

There are varying statistics given for the number of airmen killed during the Battle of Britain. The most reliable source indicates the following:

Month	Fighter Command	Luftwaffe Fighter Pilots
July (10-31)	68	52
August	176	233
September	173	191
October	120	75
Total	**537**	**551**

Source: *The Battle of Britain: Then and Now,* published by *After the Battle Magazine* (1989).

Fighter Command Survives

Fighter Command never managed to achieve air superiority in the summer and autumn of 1940, proved by the fact that air raids continued until the following May. Germany was not seriously weakened by the battle, and neither was the threat facing Britain. Hitler was still the unchallenged master of Europe, and it would take several years and the intervention of the USA before the allied armies would be strong enough to challenge the Wehrmacht.

Fighter Command certainly did not achieve victory in the conventional sense in 1940. Its victory lay simply in the fact of its survival. In order to judge the nature and significance of this victory, it is necessary to assess the danger Britain faced in 1940. Had the *Luftwaffe* succeeded in overcoming Britain's defences and establishing air superiority, would an invasion have necessarily followed?

It is certainly true that Hitler did not take a detailed personal interest in the attack on Britain as he did with his other campaigns, for example against Poland, Norway, France and Russia. Apart from commissioning the plans for Sealion and giving Goering the order to launch the different phases of the attack, he played little part. From this it might be inferred that the German leader was not serious – or perhaps in two minds about launching an invasion of Britain.

Hitler consulting with his generals in 1940. The German leader did not appear too disconcerted by his failure to defeat Britain. By early 1941, the focus of his attention had turned eastwards towards an attack on the Soviet Union.

Winston Churchill

Winston Churchill's defiant attitude and stirring speeches in 1940 inspired a nation at a time when many of his colleagues thought Britain faced certain defeat. He convinced the British people that they had won a great victory in the air, and were capable of withstanding the Blitz. He took a close interest in developments, yet he played no day-to-day role in the Battle of Britain, leaving strategy to Dowding and the Air Ministry. His interventions when they came were controversial and not always welcome: he suggested that the training period of pilots be reduced to speed up the flow of men to the squadrons. He also supported Leigh-Mallory's 'big wings' policy because the idea of shooting down the maximum number of German aircraft was more appealing to him than Dowding and Park's tactic of conserving aircraft. On the overall progress of the battle, Churchill's judgement was much more sound. He sensed that Britain had a good chance of victory once the Germans switched their main attack to London in September 1940.

weblinks
For more information on Britain's leader during World War II, go to
www.waylinks.co.uk/ worldwarsbattleofbritain

Upon becoming prime minister Winston Churchill told the House of Commons: 'I have nothing to offer but blood, toil, tears, and sweat: You ask, what is our policy? I will say: It is to wage war, by sea, land, and air, with all our might. You ask, what is our aim? I can answer in one word: Victory.' He is seen here inspecting coastal defence stations in the north east of England.

A Crucial Battle

However, Hitler was acutely aware of the dangers of an undefeated enemy lying at his rear while his forces were concentrated on the invasion of Russia. There is little doubt that, as an arch-opportunist, he would have given the go-ahead for Sealion if the *Luftwaffe* had shown signs of winning the air war, or if Britain's will to fight had shown signs of breaking during the Blitz that followed.

Even if there were no invasion threat in 1940, the Battle of Britain was no less crucial an encounter. If Fighter Command had been destroyed or neutralized, German planes would have been able to rain bombs on Britain in daylight unopposed, inflicting death and destruction on a scale that may have ultimately forced a British surrender.

'A triumph of skill'

Werner Kreipe, Chief Operations Officer, *Luftflotte* 3:

'Though the air battles over England were perhaps a triumph of skill and bravery so far as the German air crews were concerned, from the strategic point of view, it was a failure and contributed to our ultimate defeat. The decision to fight it marks a turning point in the history of the Second World War. the German air force, lacking any clear objective laid down by the Supreme Command, was bled almost to death…'

Quoted in Len Deighton, *The Battle of Britain*

A British defeat, either by this means or by invasion, would have changed the course of the war. Hitler, now unopposed in Europe, would almost certainly have invaded the Soviet Union earlier than June 1941, giving the invading forces enough time to occupy Moscow and Leningrad before the Russian winter halted their advance.

With Britain occupied, the Allies would have had no European base from which to launch an attack on Western Europe in 1944. The USA, lacking a European ally, is unlikely to have taken on Nazi Germany alone, and would have been more concerned with opposing Japanese expansion in the Pacific.

A Nazi occupation of Britain would have meant a harsh regime. A German army order of 9 September 1940 indicated their intention, once Britain had been occupied, to impose the death penalty on all opposition, and to ship able men to the continent, possibly for slave labour. Many more Jews almost certainly would have been slaughtered in the death camps.

The Battle of Britain was Hitler's first defeat of the war, and in this sense it gave an immense psychological boost to the allied cause. By facing up to the might of the *Luftwaffe*, Britain gave hope to the occupied nations of Europe. Britain's survival at this stage in the war was also a key factor in persuading Franklin Roosevelt, the US president, that Britain was worth helping. Fighter Command's efforts during the summer and autumn of 1940 allowed Britain to remain in the war at this critical time, enabling her to come back in strength with America's help in 1942.

The D-Day landings in June 1944. Britain could not have been used as a base for the reinvasion of Europe had Germany won the Battle of Britain and occupied the country.

Timeline

1936 **July** Dowding appointed head of Fighter Command. Starts organizing Britain's defences.

1939 **September** Germany invades Poland.
3 September Britain and France declare war on Germany.

1940 **8 April** Germany invades Norway and Denmark.
10 April Germany invades Holland, Belgium and Luxembourg.

10 May Germany invades France.
16 May Dowding appeals to British government not to drain Britain's stock of fighters in the attempt to save France.
26 May-4 June British and French forces retreat to Dunkirk. Under heavy attack by *Luftwaffe* they are evacuated to England.

22 June France surrenders.

10 July Battle of Britain commences with *Luftwaffe* attacks on Channel shipping.
13 July Plans for Operation Sealion – the invasion of Britain – are presented to Hitler.
16 July Hitler issues Directive 16, ordering preparation of Sealion.

12 August *Luftwaffe* attacks Britain's radar stations in an attempt to 'blind' Britain prior to *Adlerangriff* (Eagle Attack).

13 August *Adlertag* (Eagle Day): the start of a *Luftwaffe* offensive against Fighter Command itself: its airfields, radar stations, etc.
15 August Major assault by all three *Luftwaffe* air fleets. The first and last large scale raid by *Luftflotte* 5 on Britain.
20 August Churchill gives speech in Parliament giving thanks to the pilots of Fighter Command: 'Never in the field of human conflict was so much owed by so many to so few.'
24 August-6 Sept The most intense phase of the battle: a concentrated *Luftwaffe* assault on Fighter Command's airfields in the south and south east of England. During this phase, Fighter Command comes closest to being overwhelmed.
24 August Germans bomb City of London due to navigational error.
25-28 August Bomber Command launches air raids on Berlin in retaliation. Berliners shocked. Hitler is outraged.

1-3 September Large scale evacuation of children from London to homes in the countryside.
3 September Goering, with Hitler's urging, orders major daylight offensive against London.
7 September Blitz on London begins with massed raids by day and night.

Glossary

15 September The climax of the battle: Germans send their biggest raids and are still matched by Fighter Command. Arguably the day the Battle of Britain was won.
17 September Hitler postpones Operation Sealion indefinitely.
30 September *Luftwaffe* decides to withdraw almost all bombers from daylight raids.

31 October The official end date of the Battle of Britain. The Government Defence Committee chaired by the prime minister agrees that the danger of invasion has become 'relatively remote'. British anti-invasion forces are stood down from a state of 'immediate readiness'.

14 November Night-time raid by *Luftwaffe* on Coventry destroys the centre of the city.
25 November Sholto Douglas replaces Hugh Dowding as C-in-C of Fighter Command.

1941 **11 May** The end of the Blitz.

22 June Operation Barbarossa: Germany invades the USSR.

ack ack guns anti-aircraft guns.
Adlerangriff **(Eagle Attack)** this was the code name for the *Luftwaffe's* assault on Fighter Command, which began on 13 August 1940.
Adlertag **(Eagle Day)** 13 August the day that the Eagle Attack was launched.
aerodynamic designed to reduce air resistance, especially to increase fuel efficiency or speed.
air raid shelter a bomb-proof shelter for use during an attack by enemy aircraft.
Allied troops soldiers fighting for the Allies (including Britain, France, and later Russia and the USA) in World War II.
anti-aircraft gun guns designed to destroy enemy aircraft.
anti-tank ditches ditches dug across roads to prevent or delay the progress of tanks.
armada a large fleet of ships or formation of planes.
artillery guns guns with a large-diameter barrel, such as cannons.
attrition the gradual wearing away of an enemy by persistent attack.
bayonet a blade attached to the end of a rifle and used for stabbing.
beachhead a part of an enemy shoreline that troops have captured and are using as a base for launching an attack further inland.
blackout a period during wartime in which all lights are to be turned off or covered up at night to prevent towns from being seen by enemy bombers.
Blitz taken from the German word Blitzkrieg ('lightning war'), the Blitz became the term for Germany's sustained campaign of bombing British cities that lasted from September 1940 to May 1941.
Blitzkrieg German for 'lightning war'. A rapid military offensive using ground and air forces.
blockade an organized action using ships and troops designed to prevent people or goods leaving a place.
canopy the hood of an aircraft.

coastal shipping a number of ships operating out of ports along a coast.

cockpit the compartment in an aircraft where the pilot sits.

combat zone the area of battle.

convoy a group of ships (or other vehicles) travelling together.

cowling a removable metal covering for an aircraft engine.

dispersal hut a building at an RAF sector station where Fighter Command pilots waited for the order to scramble.

dogfight an aerial combat involving two or more fighter planes.

early warning system a network of sensing devices, such as radar and observer posts, designed to give advance warning of an enemy attack.

field guns mobile guns used for operations on the battlefield.

Fighter Command the branch of the RAF dedicated to the defence of Britain during World War II. It was formed in 1936 and disbanded in 1968.

fighter direction system the early warning and operations room system that directed fighter planes towards the incoming enemy aircraft.

Fliegerkorps sub groups of a *Luftwaffe* air fleet.

fuselage an aircraft's body, excluding the wings.

general staff a group of officers who aid a commander in administration, training and supply.

Geschwader subgroup of a *Luftwaffe Fliegerkorp*, consisting of about 120 aircraft made up of either bombers or fighters.

Gruppen subgroups of a *Luftwaffe Geschwader*, consisting of 36 aircraft.

Luftflotten German air fleets.

Luftwaffe the German air force.

manoeuvrable able to change course, for example, by turning, diving or climbing.

monoplane an aircraft with a single pair of wings.

munitions military supplies such as arms and ammunition.

Nazi Germany Germany between 1933 and 1945 when it was ruled by the National Socialist (Nazi) Party.

Nuremberg war crimes trial a tribunal held after the Second World War in the German city of Nuremberg to try the surviving Nazi leadership for planning and carrying out the war, and for atrocities committed in the course of it.

panzer a German armoured vehicle, especially a tank.

pillboxes small fortified shelters with a flat roof in which a large gun is sited.

propaganda organized publicity, often by a government, to promote a particular view.

radar a method of identifying the position of distant objects using radio waves.

ripcord a cord that, when pulled, opens a parachute.

Schwarm a German fighter formation, involving flying in pairs or fours.

scramble to launch a number of aircraft in a short space of time in response to an impending attack, or to be launched in these circumstances.

sector station an RAF airfield.

sortie a mission flown by a combat aircraft.

Soviet Union also known as the USSR (Union of Soviet Socialist Republics), a country formed from the territories of the Russian Empire in 1917, which lasted until 1991.

squadron a sub-group of an air force. In the case of Fighter Command, full-strength squadrons numbered 16 aircraft.

Staffel a subgroup of a *Luftwaffe Gruppe*, consisting of 12 aircraft. This was the equivalent of an RAF squadron.

transports ships used to transport troops.

Wehrmacht the German army.

Sources and Resources

Further Reading
Battle of Britain by Len Deighton (Jonathan Cape, 1980)

The Blitz by Andrew Langley (Heinemann Library, 1995)

The Battle of Britain: July-October 1940: An Oral History of Britain's 'Finest Hour' by Matthew Parker (Headline, 2000)

At Home in World War Two: The Blitz by Stewart Ross (Evans, 2001)

Battle of Britain by Chris Priestley (Scholastic, 2002)

The World Wars: Germany and Japan Attack by Sean Sheehan (Hodder Wayland, 2000)

Other Sources
The Battle of Britain: The Siege That Failed by Gerald Cole (Firefly Publications, 1990)

Nine Lives by Alan Deere and Air Chief Marshal Lord Dowding (Goodall Publications, 1999)

The Last Enemy by Richard Hillary (Pimlico, 1997)

The Battle of Britain: The Jubilee History by Richard Hough and Denis Richards (Hodder & Stoughton, 1989)

The Battle by Richard Overy (Penguin, 2000)

The Battle of Britain: Dowding and the First Victory, 1940 by John Ray (Cassell, 1994)

The Battle of Britain by John Frayn Turner (Airlife Publishing, 1998)

Places to Visit
Imperial War Museum
Lambeth Road
London SE1 6HZ
Tel: 020 7416 5000

Imperial War Museum
Duxford
Cambridgeshire, CB2 4QR
Tel: 01223 835000
Duxford was a sector station during the Battle of Britain and is now a museum dedicated to aviation. It includes 180 historic aircraft including World War I bi-planes as well as Spitfires. Many of its aeroplanes still fly.

Biggin Hill
Kent TN16 3BN
Tel: 01959 578500
Situated on the North Downs, south of London, Biggin Hill was one of the busiest sector stations during the Battle of Britain. The RAF finally left Biggin Hill in 1992, and today a number of flying clubs are situated there, and it hosts frequent spectacular air displays.

For further information about topics relevant to this book, go to
www.waylinks.co.uk/worldwarsbattleofbritain

Index